Animal Offspring

Penguins and Their Chicks

by Margaret Hall

Consulting Editor: Gail Saunders-Smith, Ph.D.
Consultant: Brete G. Griffin, Education Director
American Birding Association
Colorado Springs, Colorado

Capstone
press

Mankato, Minnesota

Pebble Plus is published by Capstone Press
151 Good Counsel Drive, P.O. Box 669, Mankato, Minnesota 56002
http://www.capstone-press.com

1 2 3 4 5 6 08 07 06 05 04 03

Library of Congress Cataloging-in-Publication Data
Hall, Margaret, 1947–
Penguins and their chicks/by Margaret Hall.
v. cm.—(Pebble plus: Animal offspring)
Includes bibliographical references (p. 23) and index.
Contents: Penguins—Eggs—Penguin chicks—Growing up—Watch penguins grow.
ISBN 0-7368-2109-0 (hardcover)
1. Penguins—Infancy—Juvenile literature. 2. Parental behavior in animals—Juvenile literature. [1. Penguins. 2. Animals—Infancy.] 1. Title.
QL696.S473 H25 2004
589.47'139—dc21   2002155654

Editorial Credits
Sarah L. Schuette, editor; Kia Adams, series designer; Jenny Schonborn, cover production designer;
    Kelly Garvin, photo researcher; Eric Kudalis, product planning editor

Photo Credits
Bruce Coleman Inc./Fritz Polking, 20 (right)
Digital Vision, cover, 1, 5
Eda Rogers, 6–7
Joe McDonald, 13
Minden Pictures/Mitsuaki Iwago, 9; Frans Lanting, 11, 17, 20 (left); Tui De Roy, 18–19
Sylvia Stevens, 14–15
Visuals Unlimited/Fritz Polking, 21 (left); Kjell B. Sandved, 21 (right)

Note to Parents and Teachers

The Animal Offspring series supports national science standards related to life science. This book describes and illustrates penguins and their chicks. The images support early readers in understanding the text. The repetition of words and phrases helps early readers learn new words. This book also introduces early readers to subject-specific vocabulary words, which are defined in the Glossary section. Early readers may need assistance to read some words and to use the Table of Contents, Glossary, Read More, Internet Sites, and Index/Word List sections of the book.

Word Count: 109
Early-Intervention Level: 12

Table of Contents

Penguins

Penguins are birds that
use their wings to swim.
They cannot fly. Young
penguins are called chicks.

Penguins come to land
to mate and lay eggs.

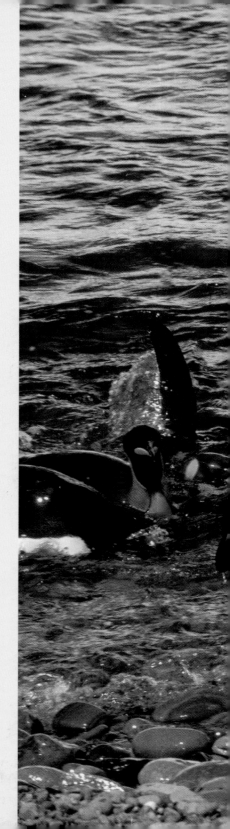

Eggs

Female penguins lay one
to three eggs. Some penguins
keep their eggs on their feet.
Other penguins keep their
eggs in a nest.

Most penguin parents take
turns keeping the eggs warm.

Penguin Chicks

A penguin chick hatches from the egg. Chicks have soft feathers called down.

Penguin parents catch fish
for the chicks to eat.

15

Sometimes the chicks stand
together to keep warm.
Chicks grow new feathers
after a few months.

Growing Up

Most penguins can swim
and take care of themselves
after about one year.

Watch Penguins Grow

hatching

adult after about five years

Glossary

bird—a warm-blooded animal with wings, two legs, and feathers; birds lay eggs; most birds can fly.

down—the soft feathers of a baby bird; young penguins with down cannot swim until they grow new feathers; the new feathers are waterproof.

hatch—to break out of an egg; a young penguin has an egg tooth on its beak; it uses the tooth to help it break the egg open.

mate—to join together to produce young; some penguins come back to the same place every year to mate.

nest—a place built to raise young; some penguins make nests; other penguins keep their young warm on their feet or by using their feathers.

wing—one of the feather-covered limbs of a bird; most birds move their wings to fly.

Read More

Guiberson, Brenda Z. *The Emperor Lays an Egg.* New York: Henry Holt, 2001.

Kendell, Patricia. *Penguins.* In the Wild. Chicago: Raintree, 2003.

Markle, Sandra. *Growing Up Wild: Penguins.* New York: Atheneum Books for Young Readers, 2001.

Trumbauer, Lisa. *The Life Cycle of a Penguin.* Life Cycles. Mankato, Minn.: Pebble Books, 2004.

Internet Sites

Do you want to find out more about penguins and their chicks? Let FactHound, our fact-finding hound dog, do the research for you.

Here's how:

1) Visit *http://www.facthound.com*

2) Type in the **Book ID** number: **0736821090**

3) Click on **FETCH IT**.

FactHound will fetch Internet sites picked by our editors just for you!

Index/Word List